# 1 IS
# FOR
# ONE

Published in the United States of America in 1996
by **MONDO Publishing**

First published in 1985 by Oxford University Press

Text copyright © 1996, 1985 by Nadia Wheatley
Illustrations copyright © 1996 by Mondo Publishing

Printed in China
First Mondo printing, February 1996
04 05 06  07  08   9 8 7 6

Designed by PCI Design Group, San Antonio, Texas

**Library of Congress Cataloging-in-Publication Data**
Wheatley, Nadia.
    1 is for one / Nadia Wheatley ; illustrated by Darius Detwiler.
       p.   cm.
    Originally published: Oxford : Oxford University Press, 1985.
    Summary: Rhyming text and illustrations follow numbers from one to ten
through changing situations in three progressively smaller books.
    ISBN 1-57255-133-X (alk. paper)
    1. Counting—Juvenile literature.  [1. Counting.]  I. Detwiler, Darius, ill.
II. Title.
QA113.W49    1996
513.2'11—dc20
[E]                                95-33231
                                           CIP
                                         AC

# Nadia Wheatley
# Illustrated by Darius Detwiler

# 1

is for one
who starts
counting for fun.

# 2

is for two
who keeps mice
in a shoe.

# 3

is for three
skating fast
by the sea.

# 4

is for four
who finds life
such a bore.

# 5

## is for five
## who is learning
## to dive.

# 6

is for six
who gets
into a fix.

# 7

is for seven
cutting stars out
for heaven.

# 8

is for eight
who leaves peas
on the plate.

# 9

## is for nine hanging clothes on the line.

# 10

is for ten
who starts
counting again.